BALTIMORE
RAVENS

BY JOSH ANDERSON

Stride

An Imprint of The Child's World®
childsworld.com

The Child's World

childsworld.com

Published by The Child's World®
800-599-READ • www.childsworld.com

Photography Credits
Cover: © Andy Lyons / Staff / Getty Images; page 1: © Africa Studio / Shutterstock; page 3: © Patrick Smith / Staff / Getty Images; page 5: © Michael Reaves / Stringer / Getty Images; page 6: © Jonathan Daniel / Stringer / Getty Images; page 9: © Andy Lyons / Staff / Getty Images; page 10: © Nick Wass / Stringer / Getty Images; page 11: © stevezmina1 / Getty Images; page 12: © Todd Olszewski / Stringer / Getty Images; page 12: © Michael Reaves / Stringer / Getty Images; page 13: © Larry French / Stringer / Getty Images; page 13: © Tim Nwachukwu / Staff / Getty Images; page 14: © Patrick Smith / Staff / Getty Images; page 15: © Doug Pensinger / Staff / Getty Images; page 16: © Dan Beineke / Stringer / Getty Images; page 16: © Joe Murphy / Stringer / Getty Images; page 17: © Harry How / Staff / Getty Images; page 17: © Jamie Squire / Staff / Getty Images; page 18: © Doug Pensinger / Staff / Getty Images; page 18: © Jonathan Daniel / Staff / Getty Images; page 19: © Tom Pennington / Staff / Getty Images; page 19: © Rob Carr / Staff / Getty Images; page 20: © Andy Lyons / Staff / Getty Images; page 20: © Wesley Hitt / Stringer / Getty Images; page 21: © Patrick Smith / Staff / Getty Images; page 21: © Rob Carr / Staff / Getty Images; page 22: © Dan Beineke / Stringer / Getty Images; page 23: © Chris Graythen / Staff / Getty Images; page 23: © stevezmina1 / Getty Images; page 25: © Al Bello / Staff / Getty Images; page 26: © Christian Petersen / Staff / Getty Images; page 29: © Jamie Squire / Staff / Getty Images

ISBN Information
9781503857728 (Reinforced Library Binding)
9781503860407 (Portable Document Format)
9781503861763 (Online Multi-user eBook)
9781503863125 (Electronic Publication)

LCCN 2021952684

Printed in the United States of America

TABLE OF CONTENTS

GO RAVENS!

The Baltimore Ravens compete in the National Football **League's** (NFL's) American Football Conference (AFC). They play in the AFC North **division**, along with the Cincinnati Bengals, Cleveland Browns, and Pittsburgh Steelers. Fans in Baltimore have been lucky! In the team's first 26 seasons, the Ravens made the **playoffs** 13 times! They've also won the **Super Bowl** both times they've made it to the big game. Let's learn more about the Ravens!

AFC NORTH DIVISION

Baltimore Ravens

Cincinnati Bengals

Cleveland Browns

Pittsburgh Steelers

MARK INGRAM (LEFT) RUSHED FOR TEN TOUCHDOWNS FOR THE RAVENS IN 2019.

BECOMING THE RAVENS

The team originally joined the NFL when the Cleveland Browns moved to Baltimore and renamed themselves the "Ravens." The team has played in Baltimore ever since. In all that time, the Ravens have often had very strong defensive players. In 2000, they won Super Bowl 35, in only their fifth season in the league. In that game, they defeated the New York Giants 34–7.

VINNY TESTAVERDE STARTED AT QUARTERBACK IN THE FIRST GAME IN RAVENS HISTORY.

BY THE NUMBERS

The Ravens
have won
TWO
Super Bowls.

SIX
division titles for
the Ravens

Only **165**
points allowed
by the Ravens'
defense in 2000—
an NFL record!

14
wins for
the Ravens
in 2019

TRENT DILFER QUARTERBACKED THE RAVENS TO VICTORY IN SUPER BOWL 35.

AFTER THEIR FIRST TWO SEASONS, THE RAVENS MOVED INTO THEIR PERMANENT HOME AT M&T BANK STADIUM.

The Ravens played their first two seasons in Baltimore, Maryland's Memorial **Stadium**. In 1998, they moved into M&T Bank Stadium. On game days, the building holds 71,000 Ravens fans. M&T Stadium is located right next to Oriole Park at Camden Yards, where Major League Baseball's Baltimore Orioles play. Because the building is so environmentally friendly, the stadium received a "Gold" rating from the US Green Building Council. It was the first existing outdoor sports stadium in the whole country to receive that honor!

We're Famous!

The Ravens are named after a famous poem! Writer Edgar Allan Poe wrote many famous works in his time. One of his most recognized poems is called "The Raven." Since he wrote "The Raven" while he was living in Baltimore, fans chose the name for their football team in 1996.

UNIFORM

PURPLE

WHITE

Truly Weird

With just over two minutes left to play in a 2013 game, the Minnesota Vikings led the Ravens 12-7. But a touchdown pass by quarterback Joe Flacco gave the Ravens the lead. Amazingly, the lead would change five times in the final two minutes and five seconds. With only four seconds left, the Ravens scored a **touchdown** and took the lead for good and won 29-26. The teams combined for 36 points in the final minutes of the game!

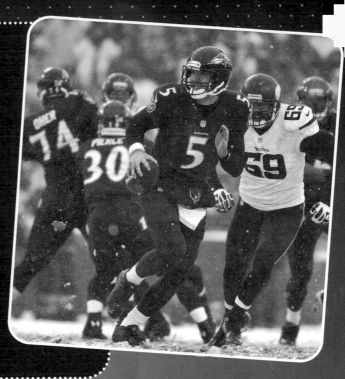

Alternate Jersey

Sometimes teams wear an alternate jersey that is different from their home and away jerseys. It might be a bright color or have a unique theme. The Ravens wore all-black uniforms for a 2020 game against the Dallas Cowboys. The uniforms proved lucky. The Ravens won 34-17.

RAVENS FANS ENJOY A DRAMATIC LIGHT SHOW AS THE TEAM IS INTRODUCED BEFORE HOME GAMES AT M&T BANK STADIUM.

Going to a game at M&T Bank Stadium can be a blast! Baltimore's Marching Ravens are a marching band that plays at every home game. They are the largest musical organization within any NFL franchise. Joining them are the Baltimore Ravens Cheerleaders, who entertain fans during breaks in the action. The team's mascot is Poe, a huge costumed raven who wears a team jersey. Hungry fans can enjoy M&T Bank Stadium's crab tots. Since Maryland is famous for its crab dishes, it's a great way to eat like a local!

POE

HEROES OF HISTORY

Jamal Lewis
Running Back | 2000–2006

Lewis played six seasons for the Ravens. He is the team's all-time leader with 7,801 rushing yards. Lewis's 2003 season is one of the best ever for a running back. That year, he rushed for 2,066 yards. That's the third most by a player in a single season!

Jonathan Ogden
Offensive Tackle | 1996–2007

Ogden was the Ravens' first-ever selection in the NFL Draft. He started 176 games for the team over 12 seasons. Ogden made the **Pro Bowl** after every season of his career except his **rookie** year. In 2013, he became the first Raven enshrined into the Pro Football **Hall of Fame**.

Ed Reed
Safety | 2002–2012

Reed is the NFL's all-time leader in interception return yards with 1,590. He also ranks seventh all-time with 64 career interceptions. Reed was named Defensive Player of the Year in 2004. He was chosen for the Pro Bowl nine times. He is a member of the Pro Football Hall of Fame.

Terrell Suggs
Linebacker | 2003–2018

Suggs ranks eighth all-time with 139 **sacks**. He finished the 2011 season with 14 sacks and seven forced fumbles. That year, he was named the league's Defensive Player of the Year. Suggs helped lead the Ravens to victory in Super Bowl 47. He was chosen for seven Pro Bowls in his career.

JANUARY 28, 2001

In their first-ever trip to the Super Bowl, the Ravens defeat the New York Giants 34–7.

The Ravens defeat the Tennessee Titans 13–10 and advance to the AFC Championship Game.

JANUARY 10, 2009

BIG DAYS

APRIL 26, 2018

Baltimore selects quarterback Lamar Jackson from the University of Louisville with the final pick of the NFL Draft's first round.

The Ravens defeat the rival Pittsburgh Steelers for the team's 14th win of the season, a franchise record.

DECEMBER 29, 2019

MODERN-DAY MARVELS

Mark Andrews
Tight End | Debut: 2018

Andrews is the only tight end in Ravens history with four seasons in which he totaled at least 700 receiving yards and seven touchdown catches. Andrews set the Ravens' single-season record in 2021 when he gained 1,361 receiving yards. He was also chosen for the Pro Bowl after the 2019 and 2021 seasons.

Marlon Humphrey
Cornerback | Debut: 2017

Before joining the Ravens, Humphrey was a star at the University of Alabama. Since being drafted by Baltimore in the first round of the 2017 NFL Draft, Humphrey has been selected for the Pro Bowl twice. His eight forced fumbles in 2020 were only two short of the NFL record.

Lamar Jackson
Quarterback | Debut: 2018

Jackson took over as the team's starter late in the 2018 season. He led the Ravens to the playoffs his first three seasons with the team. He won the league's **Most Valuable Player** (MVP) Award in 2019. That year, Jackson led the NFL with 36 touchdown passes and finished sixth with 1,206 rushing yards.

Justin Tucker
Kicker | Debut: 2012

Tucker is the NFL's all-time leader in field goal percentage. He has connected on over 90 percent of his field goal attempts during his career. In 2021, Tucker set the NFL record by kicking a 66-yard field goal—the longest ever! He's been selected for the Pro Bowl five times.

RAY LEWIS WAS SELECTED FOR 12 PRO BOWLS DURING HIS CAREER.

RAY LEWIS

Lewis anchored the Ravens defense for more than a decade and a half. He's the NFL's career leader in solo tackles with 1,568. Lewis's 2,059 combined tackles also rank first all-time. He led the Ravens to victory in two Super Bowls and was named Defensive Player of the Year twice. Lewis was chosen for the NFL's 100th Anniversary All-Time team. He is also a member of the Pro Football Hall of Fame

FAN FAVORITE

Joe Flacco–Quarterback
2008–2018

Flacco led the Ravens in 96 victories as a starting quarterback in his 11 seasons with the team. He's a beloved figure in Baltimore for his performance in Super Bowl 47, when he led the Ravens to victory over the San Francisco 49ers. Flacco threw for 212 touchdowns during his time with the team.

#1

THE BIG GAME

After their Super Bowl matchup with the San Francisco 49ers, the Ravens would be saying goodbye to legendary linebacker Ray Lewis, who was retiring from the game. The team hoped to send Lewis off with a victory in the big game. Early in the third quarter, it seemed like the Ravens might cruise to victory. But early in the fourth quarter, San Francisco cut the Ravens' lead to 31–29. In the end, Baltimore won 34–31. Lewis had seven combined tackles in the contest. Quarterback Joe Flacco was named Most Valuable Player of the game after throwing three touchdown passes.

WIDE RECEIVER ANQUAN BOLDIN HAD 104 YARDS RECEIVING FOR THE RAVENS IN SUPER BOWL 47.

COACH JOHN HARBAUGH LED
THE RAVENS TO VICTORY IN
SUPER BOWL 47.

AMAZING FEATS

36 Touchdown Passes
In 2019 by **QUARTERBACK** Lamar Jackson

14 Rushing Touchdowns
In 2003 by **RUNNING BACK** Jamal Lewis

1,361 Receiving Yards
In 2021 by **TIGHT END** Mark Andrews

17 Sacks
In 2014 by **DEFENSIVE END** Elvis Dumervil

ALL-TIME BEST

PASSING YARDS

Joe Flacco
38,245

Lamar Jackson
9,967*

Kyle Boller
7,846

RUSHING YARDS

Jamal Lewis
7,801

Ray Rice
6,180

Lamar Jackson
3,673*

RECEIVING YARDS

Derrick Mason
5,777

Todd Heap
5,492

Torrey Smith
3,591

SACKS**

Terrell Suggs
132.5

Peter Boulware
70

Michael McCrary
51

SCORING

Matt Stover
1,464

Justin Tucker
1,360*

Billy Cundiff
294

INTERCEPTIONS

Ed Reed
61

Ray Lewis
31

Chris McAlister
26

*as of 2021
**unofficial before 1982

DERRICK MASON REACHED 1,000 YARDS RECEIVING DURING FOUR OF HIS SEASONS WITH THE RAVENS.

GLOSSARY

division (dih-VIZSH-un): a group of teams within the NFL who play each other more frequently and compete for the best record

Hall of Fame (HAHL of FAYM): a museum in Canton, Ohio, that honors the best players in NFL history

league (LEEG): an organization of sports teams that compete against each other

Most Valuable Player (MOHST VALL-yuh-bul PLAY-uhr): a yearly award given to the top player in the NFL

playoffs (PLAY-ahfs): a series of games after the regular season that decides which two teams play in the Super Bowl

Pro Bowl (PRO BOWL): the NFL's All-Star game in which the best players in the league compete

rookie (RUH-kee): a player playing in his first season

sack (SAK): when a quarterback is tackled behind the line of scrimmage before he can throw the ball

stadium (STAY-dee-uhm): a building with a field and seats for fans where teams play

Super Bowl (SOO-puhr BOWL): the championship game of the NFL, played between the winners of the AFC and the NFC

touchdown (TUTCH-down): a play in which the ball is brought into the other team's end zone, resulting in six points

FIND OUT MORE

IN THE LIBRARY

Bulgar, Beth and Mark Bechtel. *My First Book of Football.*
New York, NY: Time Inc. Books, 2015.

Jacobs, Greg. *The Everything Kids' Football Book, 7th Edition*.
Avon, MA: Adams Media, 2021.

Sports Illustrated Kids. *The Greatest Football Teams of All Time*.
New York, NY: Time Inc. Books, 2018.

Wyner, Zach. *Baltimore Ravens*. New York, NY: AV2, 2020.

ON THE WEB

Visit our website for links about the Baltimore Ravens:
childsworld.com/links

Note to parents, teachers, and librarians: We routinely verify our web
links to make sure they are safe and active sites. Encourage your
readers to check them out!

INDEX

ABOUT THE AUTHOR

Josh Anderson has published over 50 books for children and young adults. His two boys are the greatest joys in his life. Hobbies include coaching his sons in youth basketball, no-holds-barred games of Apples to Apples, and taking long family walks. His favorite NFL team is a secret he'll never share!